Published in Great Britain 1976 by
Private Eye Productions Limited,
34 Greek Street, London W1.
In association with André Deutsch Limited,
105 Great Russell Street, London WC1.

(c) Pressdram Limited
SBN 233 96826 1

Designed by Peter Windett.
Printed in Great Britain by Halstan & Co. Ltd.,
Amersham, Bucks.

Book of Bores
Drawings by
Michael Heath

A Private Eye book
with André Deutsch London

ABOUT THE AUTHORS...

"Of course I know all the people at *Private Eye* I was at Cambridge with Dudley Moore and David Frost who started it and Ned Sherrin who put up the money right at the beginning we shared rooms at Brasenose I think the best thing they've ever done quite frankly are those Bores you know people rabbiting on about things they don't know anything about you remember Cynthia I showed you that marvellous one about a man at the doctor's only you didn't like it anyway I know Gerald Scarfe that's the man who does the drawings terribly well we shared a flat together back in the sixties you remember Gerald don't you Cynthia a fat red-headed chap with a beard and everybody called him Willy..."

"Hello, Simon? It's me — Arnold — remember me? I rang you up last night about my wife and how she can't go into lifts — anyway this Cyprus business — I was in Cyprus — stationed during my National Service — that's something that in my view should definitely be brought back — you never had soccer hooligans when there was National Service — you probably disagree with me anyway I think your show's terrific *PIP PIP PIP* — hello? hello? yes sorry I thought I'd run out of 2p pieces — no quite honestly since my wife died you're the only person who's showed any interest in what I've got to say. . . "

"I read about this little place in the *Guardian* it's the only pub in the Mendips where you can still get a pint of real 4-X Old Fart bitter straight from the wood what is more the barrel is mounted on special brass latchets which is the only way to make sure that the yeast remains alive if you've got time it's worth going to have a look at Fart's Brewery in Frome it's still run by the Fart family as it has been since the days of Charles I. 4-X is pretty strong, not like the fizzy muck you get in most pubs it's got a curious taste — a bit difficult to describe — but if you've ever drunk Bladder's Extra Mild or Tomlinson's Old Jubilee Stout — you'll have a vague idea of what's in store it's real beer all right and it doesn't taste at all bad if you put a dash of lime in it. . . "

"As a male your body is a blunt instrument to my impersonal flesh, your offered cigarette a symbol of rape holding the door open is for you a way of trapping me (you shit) so that you can treat me as a plaything hoping to find your crummy mother in my violated body (no way!) the female child is conditioned from birth to accept the role of an uncomplaining child-bearing machine (don't you dare patronise me!) underwear was designed by the capitalist male to enslave a woman's body well we have the Pill now we have the choice which is giving us freedom to do our thing we don't need you anymore why don't you come back to my place. . . ?"

"Terrible bloody weather guv'nor HONK
HONK what this country's coming too
VRRM VRRM VRRRMM this is it SHRIEK
SHRIEK *WHAT DO YOU THINK YOU'RE
PLAYING AT YOU F***ING STUPID
IDIOT!* VRRM shouldn't be allowed on the
roads should they guv? TOOT TOOT ZOOM
ZOOM this is it to my mind VRRM Common
Market to blame myself don't you agree guv
this is it VRRM VRRM Enoch Powell 'e
speaks 'is mind VRRM VRRM CRASH bloody
learner drivers shouldn't be allowed on the
road VRRRM VRRM VRRM I fink this is it
quite honestly sorry guv it's a One Way
I'll go back round Hyde Park Corner ZOOM
PARP the cost of living is ridiculous VRRM
VRRM. . . "

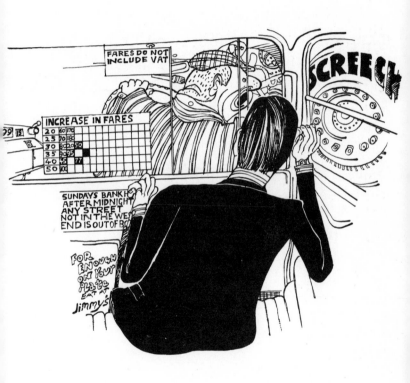

"I wonder if you've got a book a friend of mine was telling me about you know it's written by this extraordinary man who's worked out apparently that there are all these stones dotted about all over England and if you draw a line on the map if you see what I mean joining them all up it means there were people who lived millions of years ago and what this book says is that Stonehenge was some sort of Flying Saucer landing site I know it sounds incredible but apparently if you read the book you'll find it all there the awful thing is I can't remember the man's name or what the book's called but my friend said it had completely changed her life. . . "

"You should have been here this morning mate then we might have been able to help you as it is I couldn't tell you when we'll be getting any more in for a start the petrol shortage has made it impossible to forecast a delivery date and then of course there's still a backlog from the three-day week wood's in short supply and you can't get cardboard for love nor money you can go to head office mate won't make no difference they've been coming to us it's the same wherever you go mate of course now the haulage men are out there's no one to deliver them even if there was anything to deliver this is it. . . "

"The films of Franz Tuckel have for long been shamefully neglected he produced in all well over three films with such noteworthy stars as Barrington Driberg and the gorgeous Jeanette Boswell including the minor masterpiece *Hawaii Holiday* which ranks among my favourite films in which Jeanette and Barrington do the most fantastic dance routine on the top of the Statue of Liberty — breathtaking shots — and sing what is perhaps one of Sigmund Oslo's most successful duets *Forever Yours* just listen to the sweet strings of the Monty Goodman Dance Orchestra which contributed so much magic to the soundtracks of all Tuckel's screen triumphs but especially *Goodbye Manhattan* made in 1943 and never shown starring Barrington Driberg and the gorgeous Jeanette Boswell. . . "

"Christ did I shift some yesterday we started lunchtime Ian's getting married Saturday so naturally we got stuck in early I had three pints of special no four pints and two double scotches before Dave and his crowd had even bought a round and then some other bloke got hold of a crate of champagne Christ and we polished that off somehow before we went down to this club Roger knows where it was unbelievable I lost count quite frankly after the second bottle of Bacardi I don't know how I walked back to the Grapes and frankly from six o'clock onwards I can't remember much about it but apparently I managed to put away listen to this eight pints of Guinness six of Export Ales four double brandies and Christ knows what else anyway we ended up in Sheila's flat somewhere in Christ knows Maida Vale or somewhere we got through this bottle of Spanish liqueur which tasted fuckinawful quite frankly but Christ it had a hell of a kick on it apparently they had to carry me to my car Christ. . . "

"Of course Heavy Jelly has never really recovered from the loss of Rayne Fullbright I mean I respect his decision to explore new fields but a lot of the tightness has gone and though they remain one of the funkiest sounds around their new album *Brabazon Has Wings* although full of good intentions lacks the grit of the early Newcastle sound for which of course the late Bo Jabes deserves a lot of credit if you compare Dave Watson's acoustic version of *Nimble Wanker* which you can only get in the States you realise why this formerly much neglected artist has become a cult and for my money Jelly remain one of the top exponents of Wet Rock through the live albums from the Dusseldorf Farm when Noddy Grimble joined forces with T.T. White on Rhythm Bassoon. . ."

"No I had this accumulator last Wednesday at Haydock Park hang on it was Ludlow well the first one came in at 5/4 no surprise I mean it's like money in the bank when you've got Murray up on Ribena but the second race was a bit hairy Wimble's Boy just squeezed in by half a length but if there'd been ten more yards then yours truly would have been out of pocket well apart from the accumulator I had a Tote double going for me but bloody wouldn't accept my Yankee so I rang Hill's and asked for a three-way double-back Triella on the 4 o'clock as I'd won a bit of fun money on Dinky Dooble in the fifth geldings always go well when the going's sluggish but that little bugger romped home and by the end of the day I would have been quids in but bloody Piggott threw the sixth well the next day that would be Thursday. . . "

"Basically when Pam and I realised what damage we were doing to our colons by not taking enough roughage plus the fact that practically everything you buy from normal food shops is completely poisoned by the inclusion of chemical preservatives we came to the conclusion that we had to totally re-think our attitude towards body-fuel help yourself to the soya bean loaf and the idea that a big piece of dead animal flesh charred on both sides can increase your potency is ridiculous three ounces of dried wheat germ taken with a glass of free-range spring water is all the human body needs to function please have some soya bean loaf as I was saying sugar is a killer whichever way you take it pre-historic man died with all his teeth and today kids of six are having to wear dentures which is to Pam's and my way of thinking a vindication of everything we believe in are you sure you won't have the soya bean loaf it's delicious with Pam's charcoal jam. . . "

"Javanese birds are the worst I met this one the other night I'm just walking home and she pulls up in this big 1974 Chevvy, rolls the electric window down and asks me the way to Whittaker Street so I gets in cos it's obvious she's gasping for it she's giving me the come-on something rotten we get back to this place where her boyfriend's living he's not there fantastic real nympho she goes into this incredible bedroom mirrors all over the ceiling tells me to make myself a vodka and tonic all the drinks are there sherry Martini Bianco you name it anyway I go in and she's lying there in this great suspender outfit with her eyes half closed and her mouth all droopy and panting she says 'You can do what you like' did I tell you when I was in the Army in Germany there was this fantastic blonde German bird I was walking back to the Barracks one night. . . "

"No just a tonic for me yes quite sure no really I'd rather not if you don't mind you see the way I look at it is this I've given my old liver a bit of a pounding these last thirty years and I suddenly woke up one evening and asked myself do I really need it no it doesn't bother me you having one God knows how much of that stuff has swilled down my throat if I had a penny for every Scotch I've had I'd be a rich man today I tell you no I don't miss it at all it's not so much will power as common sense isn't it you ever see that thing they do with a coin and a bottle of gin it's a bit of an eye opener oh all right just to be sociable but just a small one if you insist. . . "

"The best day's work I ever did was when
I bought this freezer I won't say it was cheap
it wasn't but what you pay out on the initial
outlay you more than make up for in the long
run by buying in bulk Beryl and I go up to
this Cash'n'Carry place you know the one just
off the A24 just before you get to the Green
Shield stamp place it stands to reason I mean
you can buy a complete sheep if you want and
you're quids in they do fish fingers by the
hundredweight there again Beryl finds it a
tremendous time saver I mean if you make one
steak and kidney pie you might as well make
six that apple tart you've just eaten Beryl made
that last Easter I personally estimate that a
family of four can eat quite happily for as
little as £8 a day. . . "

"I don't normally get this one I'm usually on the 8.48 that stops at Wiggleswick Purley and Black Heath but this morning I overslept because I was so late getting back on the so-called 19.49 non-stop train due to leave at 20.15 anyway it turned out they'd cancelled it because of a points failure at Kershaw Green so I ended up having to change at Poulsden Park this is normally a good one to get it gets you in to London Bridge at 10.41 but today because they've closed the tunnel at Maudling (South) to do repair work we'll have to change at Corbett Woodall and get on the 11.07 which is coming up from Bournemouth due into Waterloo at 12.14 she's usually on time so we'l have to look sharpish as I don't expect they'll wait for connecting passengers failing that there won't be another one through till 12.05 and that's a stopper. . . "

"Now look squire why don't you push off home and forget about it I've told you before if it was up to me it would be a different story and that kind of language won't get you anywhere look it's not me that makes the rules I just work here you can write letters to who you want I'm not stopping you I understand your point of view you've come a long way but if I was to let in anyone I felt sorry for it would be more than my job's worth so why don't you run along look I don't care who you are you could be bloody Aristotle Onassis it wouldn't make no difference I'm just doing my job we've all got a job to do now don't you threaten violence on me I'm not responsible for the rules I'm just doing my job. . ."

"Did you see that programme last night blood
terrifying it's incredible apparently these
scientists in Sweden or Norway or somewhere
have discovered that certain you know anyway
apparently there are these rats and you know
pests that have over the years absorbed so
many chemicals it's bloody frightening this
film showed I mean in America they've got
these Colorado beetles but much larger and
they're virtually indestructible and this
scientist predicts that in 20 years time say it
will be virtually impossible to destroy these
er as I say you know these beetles can eat mor
food than bodyweight or something I mean
it's bloody frightening. . . "

"There was this friend of mine who's just got back from a fortnight's camping holiday in Majorca he was telling me they stopped just for a glass of lager in Dieppe on the way through that was just him and his wife and the eight children and he said it came to eighty-nine francs and the day he got there the franc came down from forty-five to the pound I think it was to three-fifty and in Italy apparently it was even more fantastic he just wanted to send this one postcard to his mates at work and he said it cost him four hundred and three lire eight pesetas for the stamp which apparently works out at something in the region of nine pounds fifty which is just incredible for a stamp I mean we complain about inflation at home but it's nothing to what they've got over there. . . "

"Flat as a millpond all the way across through the customs no problems then it was 130 all the way to just outside Pietons never touched the gear stick once fantastic lunch and then it was foot on the floor for six solid hours bloody fantastic those French roads I mean I wouldn't give you twopence for a Frenchman miserable looking bastards in my opinion but by Christ they can put a road in for you I'm telling you you don't know what six litres and an overhead cam can mean until you're out there on the Nationale really fantastic what we do is miss the Krautkopfs coming out of Chambourcy take like their equivalent of the B road down as far as Poids Lourds and then cut back along the 314 to Byrrh and then it's boom boom right down to the frontier no way. . . ."

"Of course the 1969 Koussevitsky Brahms Two has been deleted so for that matter has the Leinsdorf Vienna Volkspopper Five which was to my mind the definitive recording and I suppose the only·thing to touch Leinsdorf at his peak were the 1938 Furtwangler Berlin Radio Transcriptions that Nixa put out after the war I've got six of those they must be worth a fortune now you can't get them for love nor money I've also got the early Busch Razumovsky set which is far and away superio even to the 60's Amadeus on Heliodor which you can't get in this country which I've also got as well as Rachmaninov's Third which is not my cup of tea normally but it's amazing what a conductor like the young Karel Ancel makes of it the Czech Philharmonic make it a different work entirely I also have them with Kreisler doing Mendelsohn what an incredible fellow Kreisler was do you know apparently he. . ."

"Anyway Dad there's this man the one who had the brain of this thing from space put in him and these men who want to take over the world try to get rid of him by blasting him with this special sort of Ray Gun they've made oh yes I forgot you see you can't kill him with anything because he was put together by this doctor it was on last week's programme about this doctor who wanted to save the world from all evil and these men who are trying to destroy the world they fire off this fantastic rocket but before that happens you see the doctor has got this amazing new machine that can kill all these giant ants that are going to eat up everything it's really great. . . "

"I'll tell you five interesting things about what's happening in Portugal one that Melo Antunes played into the hands of the CIA and the worst group in the Oporto hierarchy when he couldn't see that the undercover fascists of CDS and the so-called PPD could only be crushed by the Gonzales faction of PCP who had grasped right from the start that a so-called GPC infantile leftist breakaway was playing into the hands of elements who pretended that when the Archbishop of Braga had his trousers removed by the customs men searching for illegal currency this was a quite correct expression of working-class fury at the attempt by elements of the PMG petit-bourgeoisie to smash Cunhal's efforts to reform cadres within the non-commissioned elements of COPCON who had correctly spotted that FEC, a Maoist organisation which is hysterically opposed to the CPC had played into the hands of the CIA and the worst group in the Oporto hierarchy when. . . "

"Good day to you sir I wonder if we might have a few *important* words with you about *the truth of life* and give you a chance to read our literature which contains *all* the answers to life's *problems* why we have wars and stress and spots before the eyes as is written 'and the lean and the ill favoured kine did eat up the first seven fat kine and so he spake saying' now if we might talk further I'd like to explain our first one hundred principles so that you may join us in the chosen world hereafter and receive *everlasting peace* have you ever wondered why so-called scientists say that this old earth of ours is round when we know that it is flat with elephants holding it up at each corner? have you ever wondered why the sun is blue? remember when you join us we will come around every day until the end of the world which is by the way Tuesday week at 3 p.m. . . . . "

". . . and it was reported that no one was seriously injured meanwhile in Buenos Aires there is no news of the kidnapped Czech anthropologist Dr Tibor Weeterbicz who is being held by members of the P.B.N. Peron separatist movement demanding the release of five political prisoners in Milan the deadline set for the execution of the three bank hostages held by armed gunmen expires at noon today back home there is still no further news concerning the whereabouts of Dr Gunter Cabwallander the Belgian industrialist missing from his home since last Friday police believe that break-away members of the S.H.F. splinter group are responsible news is just coming in that the Swedish consular official Mr Gottløb Nøgstrum held hostage by members of the Borneo Liberation Front for the last three years is to be released after conciliation moves by UN officials meanwhile there is still no news of the fifty two. . . "

". . . more than ever today the educational ethos is geared to perpetuate the totally out-moded concepts of old fashioned elitist bourgeois oriented society which are complete-ly meaningless within a modern classroom situation therefore the true relationship vis-a-vis pupil and teacher must relate to situat-ions which lie outside the meaningless rituals of exam oriented syllabi and which can by their basic nature trigger off a valid response in a primarily working class study-collective for example the struggle in Portugal the plight of the Shrewsbury Two the brutal suppression of workers by the Chilean junta to name but one. . . "

". . . that last bomb was a narrow escape for me I can tell you I had a dentist appointment at exactly the time the bomb went off well not exactly that time about an hour earlier but the day before the explosion the dentist rang to say could I come the following day but if he hadn't I would have been walking through Brunswick Gardens at just about the time the bomb went off and if it had been the day before I reckon I would have been a gonner that is if I'd come through Connaught Square which normally I don't do but just supposing I had gone that way I. . . "

"70p for five pounds of potatoes yer I know terrible init four bananas that'll be 90p OK? I don't know how some of these old dears live on their pensions the cost of living bein' what it is now luv what about some nice apples 10p each I know it's wicked I don't know how people manage any more quarter of mush-rooms I never sell less than half 59p bloody shocking I agree with you how about a nice salad for the old man? I've got half a cucumber for 79p yes where's it all going to end I ask myself disgraceful madam to my mind money goes nowhere these days does it? that'll be £7.95½p. . . "

"Oh no I never watch television these days it's such a waste of time I mean did you see that programme the other night with that chap Frost who interviews people absolutely dreadful my god if one can't think of anything better to do with one's time that sit glued to this sort of nonsense I was watching that programme on Tuesday about battered mothers it was complete rubbish I don't know why people can't think of something better to do with their spare time than sit in front of the box watching second-rate rubbish like *Upstairs Downstairs* did you see Sunday's episode it reached a new low I thought then there was that idiot last night..."

"You really must go and see it it's the most marvellous play I've ever seen it's so funny it's brilliant honestly I can't tell you Nigel and I just fell about it's impossible to explain you have to go and see it for yourself but you know all these people come into it like Lenin and you know James Joyce and Hitler and the way he sort of mixes them all up is absolutely brilliant I think he's terribly. . . "

"Well let me tell you that I know Lucan is actually alive and living in Toronto I got this first hand from a friend who knew Lucky very well at Eton and he knows this woman who actually saw him in a restaurant in Venice last year obviously he had shaved his beard off but it was definitely him there's no doubt about that and apparently he's got a bank account in Rhodesia you only have to have a number for that I shouldn't be telling you this but I saw him myself a few months ago I was in a pub in Budleigh Salterten and this chap bumps into me turns round to apologise and it was him obviously disguised but it was definitely him he was bald five foot six with a big scar across his nose he took one look at me and we both knew but I didn't say a word to anyone it's not a thing I would dream of telling a stranger. . . "

"It's fantastic there are queues a mile long all round the cinema I've never seen anything like it a friend of ours got in and apparently you know it's really unbelievable it's so realistic you know apparently people really do jump out of their seats when the shark comes out of the water I mean my friend you know he's seen hundreds of films and he admitted that he was really sweating when this girl was swimming in the water and then there's this other bit he told me about when this man. . ."

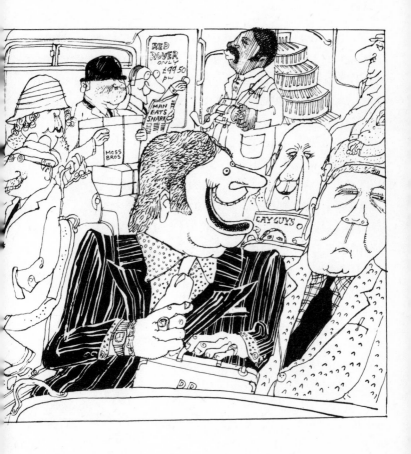

". . . no wait a minute sir take back the fiver and give me the 3p no let's start again guv'nor what did I say it was? £1.28 and you gave me two pound notes no a fiver that's it now let's do it the easy way I give you two 10ps and you give me the pound note and the shilling no what am I talking about? let's do it this way you want £3.48 change? that 50p in your hand's mine right? you give it me back OK? that's £1.50 right? now all I owe you is. . . no hang on a minute no let's go back to the beginning. . . "

". . . there's two minutes before the news so I've just got time to tell you something about tonight's Radio Three production in the *Drama Today* series it's Mrs Norris and the Angel by Antonia Maelstrom who describes the play as a tragi-comedy centring round the arrival of a circus clown at the suburban home of a retired colonel and his epileptic daughter forcing them to readjust their preconceived ideas about twentieth century society and at the same time come to terms with the semi-invalid dwarf who lives next door with his retarded step-mother an enigmatic personality who spends much of her life eating leaves and reading Swinburne's poetry was she a friend of Hitler's? that's tonight's *Drama Now* presentation at 8 o'clock PIP PIP PIP. . . "

". . . absolutely frightful the price of a telephone call these days I know it's outrageous
isn't it I mean if it goes on like this no one
will ever be able to make a call ever again
I know it's scandalous we just had our bill in
for the last quarter yes oh did you yes well
ours was £178 something or other yes Nigel
says if it goes on like this we'll have to get rid
of the thing I mean what's the point of having
a telephone if every time you pick up the
receiver it costs you something like 20p it's
not as if I ever use the thing anyway my dear
I knew there was something I've been meaning
to tell you you know that fabulous man you
met at the Rossiters' party well according to
Jocelyn he used to be a boyfriend of guess
who. . . "

"Lavinia and I have put our names down for an allotment there's a tremendously long waiting list apparently but with any luck we should be in by Christmas and then it's back to the soil for the pair of us apparently you can buy these beans from Argentina or somewhere and just a few rows give you enough protein to last you a fortnight then Lavinia wants to try her hand at courgettes you can't go wrong with courgettes can you darling? and what's that other stuff that the Rossiters have got in their window boxes you know those small things like potatoes you dry them and put them in soup anyway the local brewery sold us this barrel and you drill holes in it and then you can grow this stuff out of it and of course the beauty of this allotment is it's only 40 minutes away in the car and at £30 a year it's an absolute gift I've got this new book that's just come out which tells you what to do which has got fabulous photographs of peas and cabbages and so on. . ."

"I know exactly how you feel I used to have trouble with *my* back I still get it now and again if I do any heavy lifting or anything like that there's no use your going to your local GP all he'll do is give you aspros and tell you to take it easy did you know that your spine is like a bicycle chain and there are literally hundreds of bones all locked together and it only needs one of these to get shifted a fraction of an inch for the whole system to break down if you like I'll give you the name of the man I go to in Harley Street who specialises in this sort of thing all this bloke does is sort of yank your neck off your head and you walk out feeling a new man there are people coming to see him from literally all over the world just the other day I was in there and there was that Dr Who chappie there with some kind of back trouble. . . "

"Of course bringing in Kellogg into the mid-field was a fatal error especially when you consider the blokes they had sitting on the subs bench blokes like Gaffey and Tutt I mean four three three is alright for the big boys Real and Dynamo perfected it but quite honestly it was never going to work at Wembley I could see the goal coming before they even started they gave Boswell so much room he only had to tap the ball and that was it no way was it a great match I thought myself it was a non-game quite frankly admittedly we saw occasional flashes of Mike Letraset's brilliance as a striker but not enough to warrant his £300,000 tag but you know that's football I mean bringing in Kellogg into the midfield. . . "

"I like it very much it's terrific and I think you've got some wonderful material together and I love the drawings the drawings are super and Andre loves the drawings too but we none of us are quite sure whether it's going to work as a book and this is what we are talking about I mean independently they're very funny I mean this one here's terrific and I loved that one you know the one I can never remember jokes but anyway Michael why don't you take them all home and sort through them and meanwhile we'll mull it over at this end and then why don't we get together for lunch let's see I'm going away until the end of October so it's hopeless trying to think of it for this Christmas but anyway let's have lunch when we've all thought about it a bit more but Andre agrees we've got the makings of a really good spy thriller here once we've um er decided what we're trying to say with Bores. . . "